A New Tune A Day™
for Flute
Book 2

Published by
Boston Music Company

Edited by David Harrison
Flute adviser Alison Hayhurst
Music processed by Paul Ewers Music Design
Original compositions and arrangements by Ned Bennett
Cover and book designed by Chloë Alexander
Photography by Matthew Ward
Model: Sacha Haworth
Backing tracks by Guy Dagul
Audio performance by Alison Hayhurst
Audio recorded, mixed and mastered by Jonas Persson and John Rose

Your Guarantee of Quality
As publishers, we strive to produce every book to the highest commercial
standards. The music has been freshly engraved and the book has been
carefully designed to minimise awkward page turns and to make playing
from it a real pleasure. Throughout, the printing and binding have been
planned to ensure a sturdy, attractive publication which should give years
of enjoyment. If your copy fails to meet our high standards, please inform
us and we will gladly replace it.

To access companion recorded performances and backing tracks, visit:
www.halleonard.com/mylibrary

Enter Code
8312-1176-3715-7917

ISBN 978-1-70512-701-8

THE BOSTON MUSIC COMPANY

DISTRIBUTED BY

HAL•LEONARD®

This book © Copyright 2007 Boston Music Company
International Copyright Secured All Rights Reserved

No part of this publication may be reproduced in any form or by
any means without the prior written permission of the Publisher.

Visit Hal Leonard Online at
www.halleonard.com

T0025446

World headquarters, contact:
Hal Leonard
7777 West Bluemound Road
Milwaukee, WI 53213
Email: info@halleonard.com

In Europe, contact:
Hal Leonard Europe Limited
1 Red Place
London, W1K 6PL
Email: info@halleonardeurope.com

In Australia, contact:
Hal Leonard Australia Pty. Ltd.
4 Lentara Court
Cheltenham, Victoria, 3192 Australia
Email: info@halleonard.com.au

Lesson 21 goals:

1. The note B♭ using the thumb
2. Semiquavers

The note B♭ using the thumb key

This is a convenient way of playing B♭ and can be used when playing scales and pieces with flats in the key signature, for example F major, G minor etc.

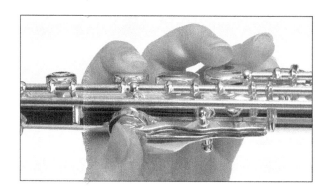

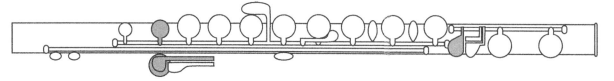

Exercise 1:

Keep your thumb on the B♭ key except when playing C.

Semiquavers

You should already be familiar with notes that last four beats (semibreve), two beats (minim), one beat (crotchet) and half a beat (quaver).

Single semiquaver and a semiquaver rest

Group of four semiquavers (worth one crotchet)

One bar of semiquavers in 4/4 time

Semiquavers are notes that last for *quarter* the length of a crotchet or *half* the length of a quaver.

Exercise 2: Double Or Quit!

Keep the beat steady and don't start too quickly. Use thumb B♭ here.

Exercise 3: Three beats per bar

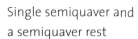

Pieces for Lesson 21

Ballad

Ned Bennett

A ballad is a slow jazz piece. Don't *swing* the quavers.

2-3

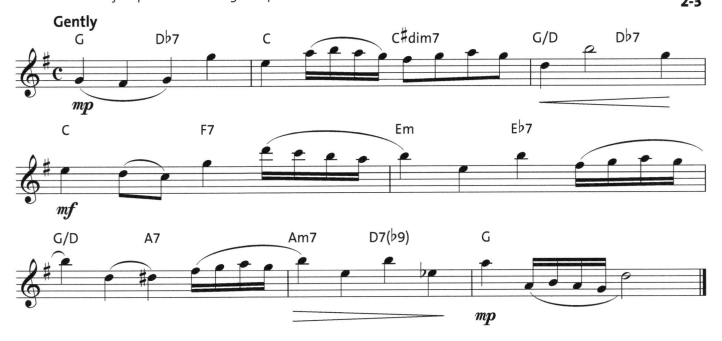

Surprise Symphony (excerpt)

Haydn

The surprise is in the 8th bar of this famous piece. Legend has it that the composer knew that his employer,
Count Esterhazy, often fell asleep during concerts. The sudden loud note was to wake him up!

4

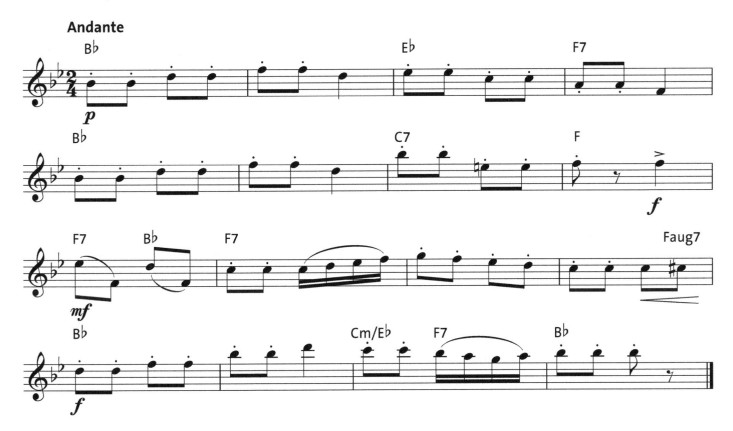

Pieces for Lesson 21

Dracula's Dance

Ned Bennett

5-6

Semiquavers can look scary at first. Practise this very slowly making sure that your minims, crotchets, quavers and semiquavers are played in tempo.

Allegro

goals:

1. **The notes top E♭ and top F**
2. **Semiquaver groups**

Top E♭

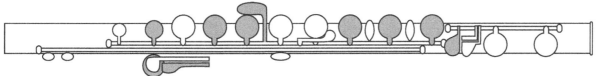

For these notes try aiming the air upwards by pushing your bottom lip forward a touch, and don't rely on blowing too hard.

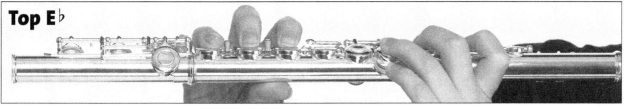

Top F

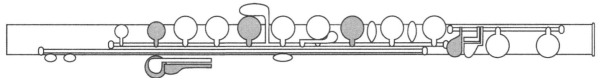

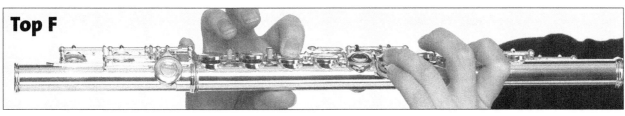

Exercise 1:

E♭ major arpeggio. All E♭s are fingered differently.

F major arpeggio.

In the exercises and pieces of the previous lesson, all the semiquavers were in groups of four lasting one beat in total. Try to learn these new patterns as rhythmic words rather than trying to count them each time.

These three combinations of quavers and semiquavers are each grouped into a crotchet's worth of notes.

 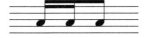 

Exercise 2:

Exercise 3:

Exercise 4:

5

Pieces for Lesson 22

Simple Gifts

Joseph Bracket Jr.

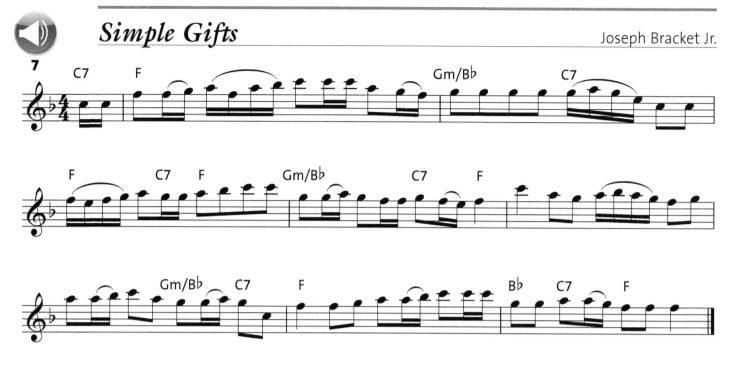

Frith Street Rag

Ned Bennett

Remember to read the grouped notes as *rhythmic words.*

Pieces for Lesson 22

Dance Of The Swans

Tchaikovsky

10-11

> ### TEMPO TERMS
>
> There are a number of articulation markings in this piece including staccato, tenuto and accent markings.
>
> They occur early in the piece, but you must apply the same articulation later on, even if none is marked, in order to achieve a consistent performance.
>
> **Allegretto** means 'a little *Allegro*',
> being somewhere between **Andante** and **Allegro** in tempo.

goals:

Lesson 23

1. **'Dotted pairs'**
2. **Scale revision**
3. **'Scotch snap'**

Dotted pairs

The 'dotted pair' is a very common rhythm: a dotted quaver (worth three semiquavers) followed by a semiquaver. Look at these three examples:

The first note of each pair is three times longer than the second. In the final example, the dotted quaver is worth 3 semiquavers. The final semiquaver completes the group (worth one crotchet in total.)

Exercise 1:

It is very important to keep the 3:1 ratio between the dotted pairs, otherwise they could sound like swing quavers which are played in a lazier way (more like 2:1).

Exercise 2:

Try playing this entire exercise in tempo. Professional musicians often practise scales in this rhythm as it helps develop coordination between the tongue and the fingers.

The Scotch snap

The Scotch snap is the opposite to the dotted pair.
The semiquaver comes first, then the dotted quaver:

Exercise 3:

Here is the scale of E♭ major written in 'Scotch snap' rhythm.

Try this for any of the scales you have learned so far.

Pieces for Lesson 23

Prelude

Chopin

12

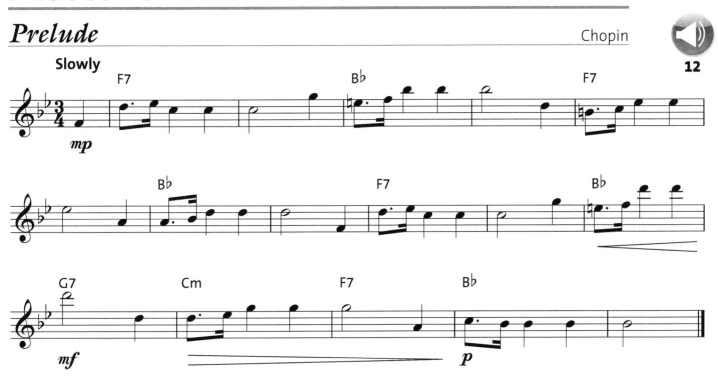

Loch Lomond

Scottish traditional

13

Watch out for the Scotch snaps in this one!

Pieces for Lesson 23

14-15

Humoresque

Dvořák

The dotted pairs here are grouped to show each half bar or minim's-worth. Make sure you don't swing this piece. Keep the dotted pairs light and accurate.

goals:

1. **The note top G**
2. **Playing in tune**
3. **Semiquavers in 6/8**

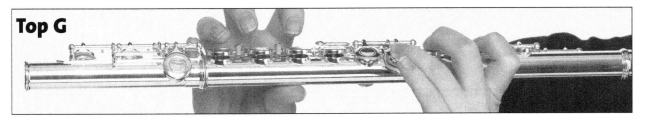

Top G

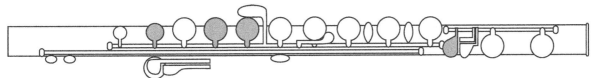

Exercise 1:

Remember to direct the air slightly upwards for the higher notes.

Intonation: playing in tune

In order to play perfectly in tune, a skilled flautist will make very small adjustments to the embouchure to lower or raise notes by minuscule amounts. These adjustments must be automatic otherwise you will have too much to think about when you are playing a piece.

Intonation is the word for tuning individual notes. Good intonation takes a while to achieve. Play this exercise at least three times a week.

Exercise 2:

Make sure you have *warmed up* your flute.

Play a long A (middle octave). Make sure you are perfectly in tune with the piano or CD.

If you are sharp (too high), pull your headjoint out a little.

Do the opposite if you are flat (too low). Your teacher will be able to guide you.

Now play the following music (in tune), in unison with the CD or piano, listening very carefully to every note. If you are in tune, the note will sound pure. If you are sharp, there will be an uncomfortable, grating sound.

To raise (sharpen) the pitch, direct the air upwards using the bottom lip.

To lower (flatten) the pitch direct the air slightly downwards into the hole.

16

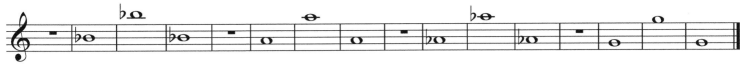

11

Lesson 24

Semiquavers in 6/8 time

Below are pairs of semiquavers within a half-bar of 6/8. As you did with the simple time groups, try to learn these rhythms as words. They have been labelled A to J.

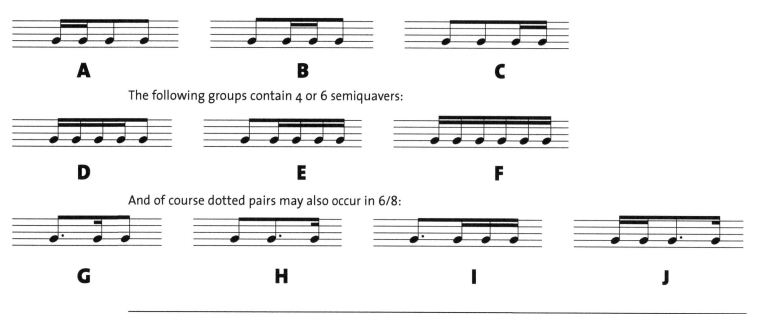

Exercise 2: Combining the groups

Choose a series of 8 groups at random and write it down. Then clap the rhythm that the groups produce.

As each group contains three quavers worth of notes, your piece will be four bars long in 6/8.

Here is an example:

Pieces for Lesson 24

Greensleeves

Attrib. Henry VIII

17

A well-known melody for practice at playing dotted pairs in 6/8 time. Are you playing the high notes in tune?

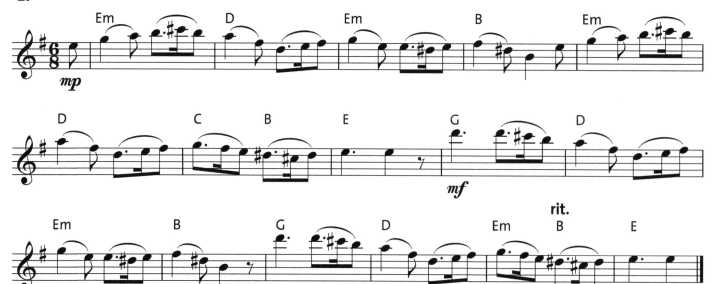

Pieces for Lesson 24

Lillabullero

17th Century

The BBC World Service used this until recently as its identification tune. "This is London…"

18-19

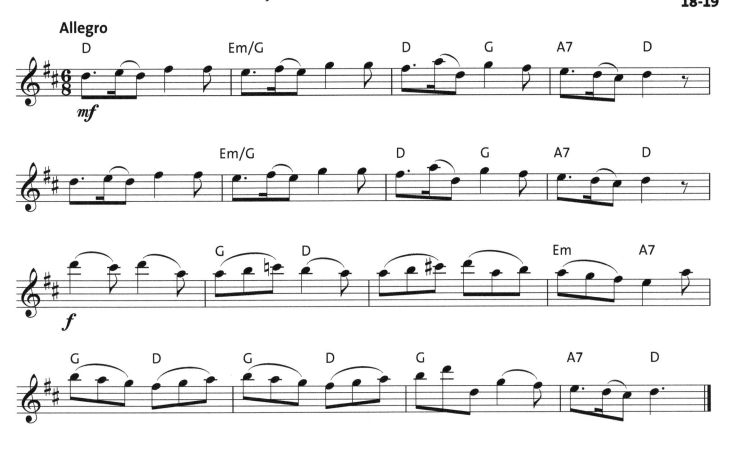

Allegro Moderato

Justano Bardi

20-21

The chromatic scale

Chromatic literally means coloured. The chromatic scale is coloured by every note that can be played on your instrument. Each note is one semitone above or below the last one.

Exercise 1:

Play one octave of the chromatic scale starting on F, ascending and descending.
You will find it is best to use the 'long' B♭ fingering when needed..

Exercise 2:

Now play the chromatic scale starting on G.

Did you notice that this uses exactly the same notes? You can start and finish the chromatic scale wherever you like, but the notes will always be the same.

Exercise 3:

Here is a chromatic scale to improve your *high* notes. Play the repeated bars many times over, slowly at first.
Keep your fingers close to the flute. Don't forget to check your *intonation*.

Exercise 4:

Another chromatic exercise to help improve your *low* notes.
You will need a strong right hand little finger for this.

Pieces for Lesson 25

When And Where

Ned Bennett

You should learn both parts. Good intonation is vital to make this piece work.

Watch out for chromatic passages.

Pieces for Lesson 25

22-23

Spring Song

Mendelssohn

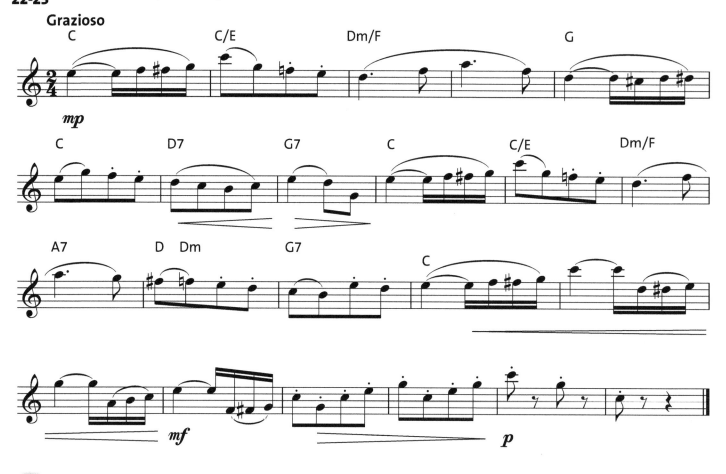

24-25

Entry Of The Gladiators

Fučík

This famous tune will need slow practice to work out the notes. Don't lose patience...it's well worth the effort!

goals:

1. The Blues scale
2. Improvisation

The Blues scale

The Blues is a style of music that originated in the southern part of the United States of America during the beginning of the 20th century.

Originally a Blues musician would sing while accompanying himself on guitar but, from the 1920s, the Blues was played on piano, saxophone, trumpet and most jazz instruments.

Most of the melodic content of the Blues uses the Blues scale, a series of notes that gives the music its special character.

Huddie Ledbetter (Leadbelly)

Exercise 1:

There is a Blues scale for every key. Here is the Blues scale in G.

Exercise 2:

Here is a short melody to illustrate how the notes of the Blues scale can sound.
Notice that you can extend the scale above and below the key notes.

Improvisation

One very essential part of Blues (and Jazz) is *improvisation*. This means that the musician makes up the melody as he or she goes along. The Blues scale makes this quite easy, as it will fit with all the different chords that accompany the Blues.

Exercise 3:

Make sure you have practised the G Blues scale so that you can play it without looking.
Play the following four bars. Can't see any notes? Then you'll have to make something up as you go along, but keep the tempo steady!

Pieces for Lesson 26

26-27

Holy-Moly Blues

Ned Bennett

Play the notated bars as written. Improvise the blank bars using only the notes of the G Blues scale.
The slashes indicate the beats in these improvised bars. If you can't think of anything to play, either repeat the
notated bar you have just played, or don't play at all...rests are a very important part of all music!

28-29

Play This Funky Music

Ned Bennett

Funk is a more modern style than Blues, although it shares many characteristics. Don't swing the quavers, and
remember to take the *D.C. al Fine* after your improvisation. Sixteen bars may seem like a long time, but it will
be over before you know it.

Exercise 4:

Here is the Blues scale in D, ascending and descending over 2 octaves.

Make sure you can play it fluently and from memory before attempting the next piece.

Alabama Boogie-Woogie

Ned Bennett

30

Boogie-Woogie was originally a style of Blues played on the piano. The left hand would play a repeated rhythm throughout that gave the music its driving nature.

Traditional Blues uses a 12-bar chord sequence to tie the music together.

This piece follows the 12-bar Blues form. Play the 'head' (melody), then two choruses of improvisation, then the head once more, remembering to go to the Coda to finish.

goals:

1. Triplet quavers
2. The note top E

Triplet quavers

Triplets are a set of three notes that occupy the time that would normally be taken up by two notes of the same value. Look at the following comparison.

Each of the three groups contains notes that add up to one crotchet. Triplet quavers (a group of three quavers with a '3' written above or below) must be played faster than ordinary quavers, but not as fast at semiquavers.

Exercise 1:

Play this with a slow and steady beat. Putting a slight accent on the notes that coincide with a beat, you should find that the triplets sort themselves out.

Count: *1 2 3 4   1   2   3   4   1   2   3   4   1   2   3   4   1...*

Exercise 2: Quavers and triplet quavers

It is easy to make the mistake of playing triplets as a group of two semiquavers followed by a quaver. Make sure all three notes are exactly the same length. Try this tongued and slurred as indicated.

The note top E

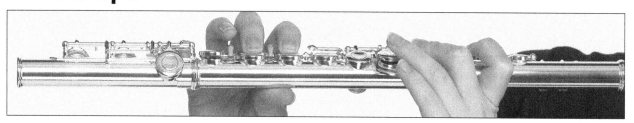

Exercise 3:

The scale and arpeggio of E minor

Pieces for Lesson 27

La donna è mobile from *Rigoletto*
Verdi

Here's a very jolly tune from a very sad opera. Make sure the dotted pairs are exact.

Barry O'Flynn
Irish Folk Song

The instruction 'with a swing' actually makes this piece easier. Like Jazz, many Irish tunes are written down in the way that's easiest to read.

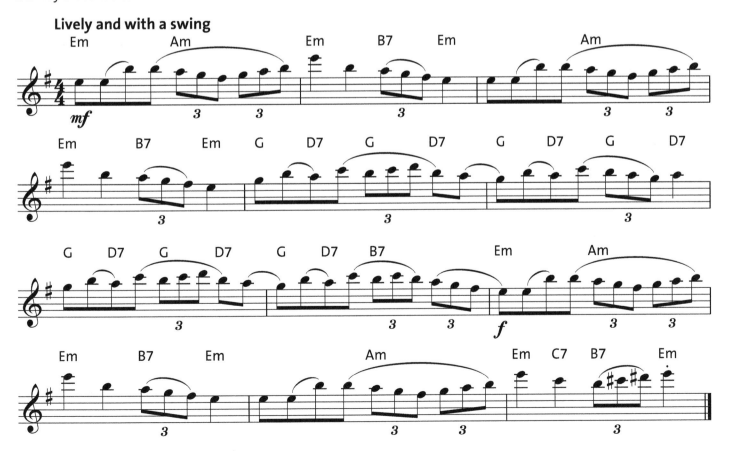

Pieces for Lesson 27

34-35

Valse No. 9 (Op. 69, No. 1)

Chopin

Chopin wrote many extremely fast pieces for piano. However, some of his most beautiful music is slow and lyrical. This must be played exactly as written. Although it looks hard, there is a lot of repetition, and remember: *lento* means 'slowly', which will help.

goals:

1. Triplet crotchets
2. Acciaccaturas

Triplet crotchets

Just as three triplet quavers occupy the space of two regular quavers, three triplet crotchets fit into the space of two ordinary crotchets.

Count: 1   2   3   4   1   2   3   4

You can see the difficulty here is that while the first note of each group of triplets falls on a beat, the second and third fall either side of the next beat.

Exercise 1:

Play both of the following. What do you notice?

Exercise 2:

The accents are there to help you because they always coincide with beats 1 and 3.
Be careful not to play triplet crotchets as a quaver-crotchet-quaver rhythm.

Acciaccatura

This is a very long word for an extremely short note. An acciaccatura (pronounced atch-akka-tour-a) may be written as a small quaver or a semiquaver with a slash through the tail, but should last no time at all and be slurred to the main note. Whether the acciaccatura comes *just before* the beat or right on it is a topic of hot debate in classical circles: let your sense of style and phrasing be your guide!

Exercise 3:

Pieces for Lesson 28

Triplet Trouble Blues

Ned Bennett

36-37

Take this slowly, but still play the acciaccaturas quickly and on the beat, not before.

Slow Blues

To The Spring

Edvard Grieg

38

Listen to the four crotchet count-in very carefully. The accompaniment consists of triplet crotchets which may put you off!

Moderato cantabile

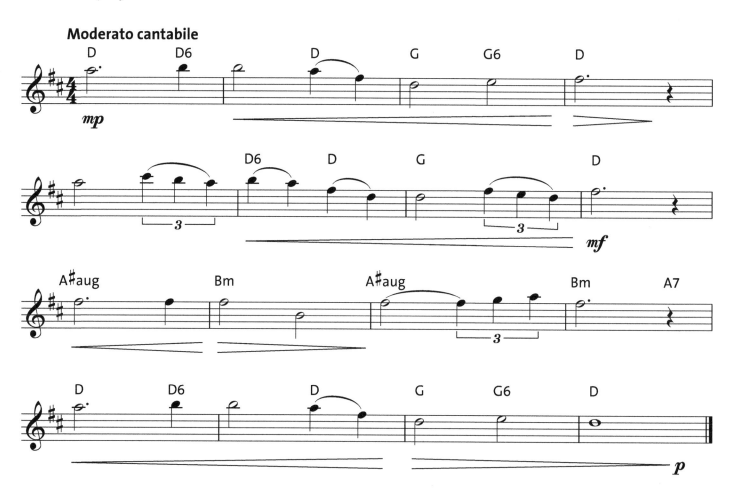

A New Tune A Day *for* Flute
Pull-out Fingering Chart

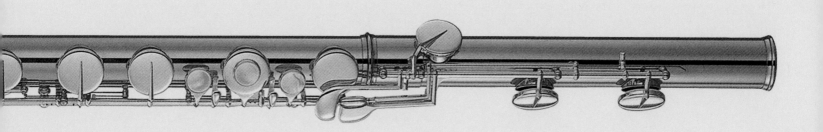

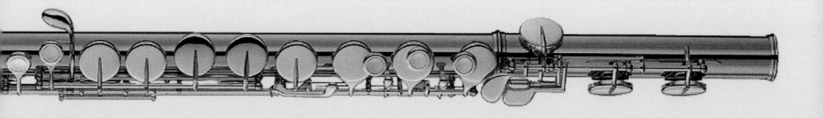

Piccolo

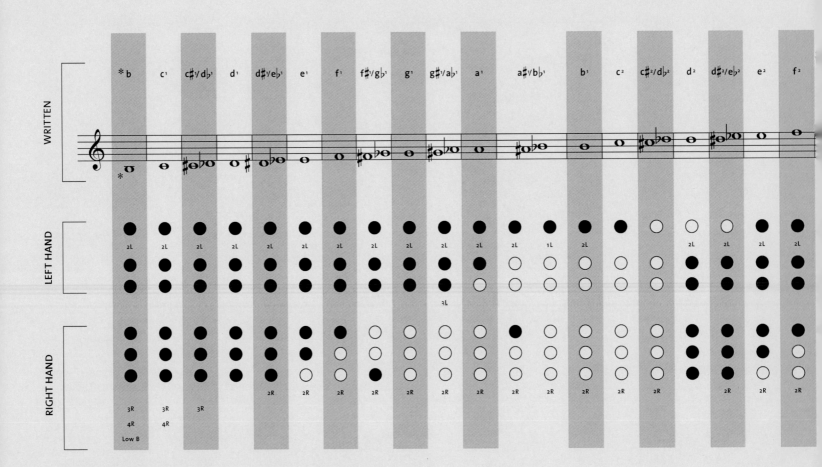

*This note can only be played on flutes with a low B key

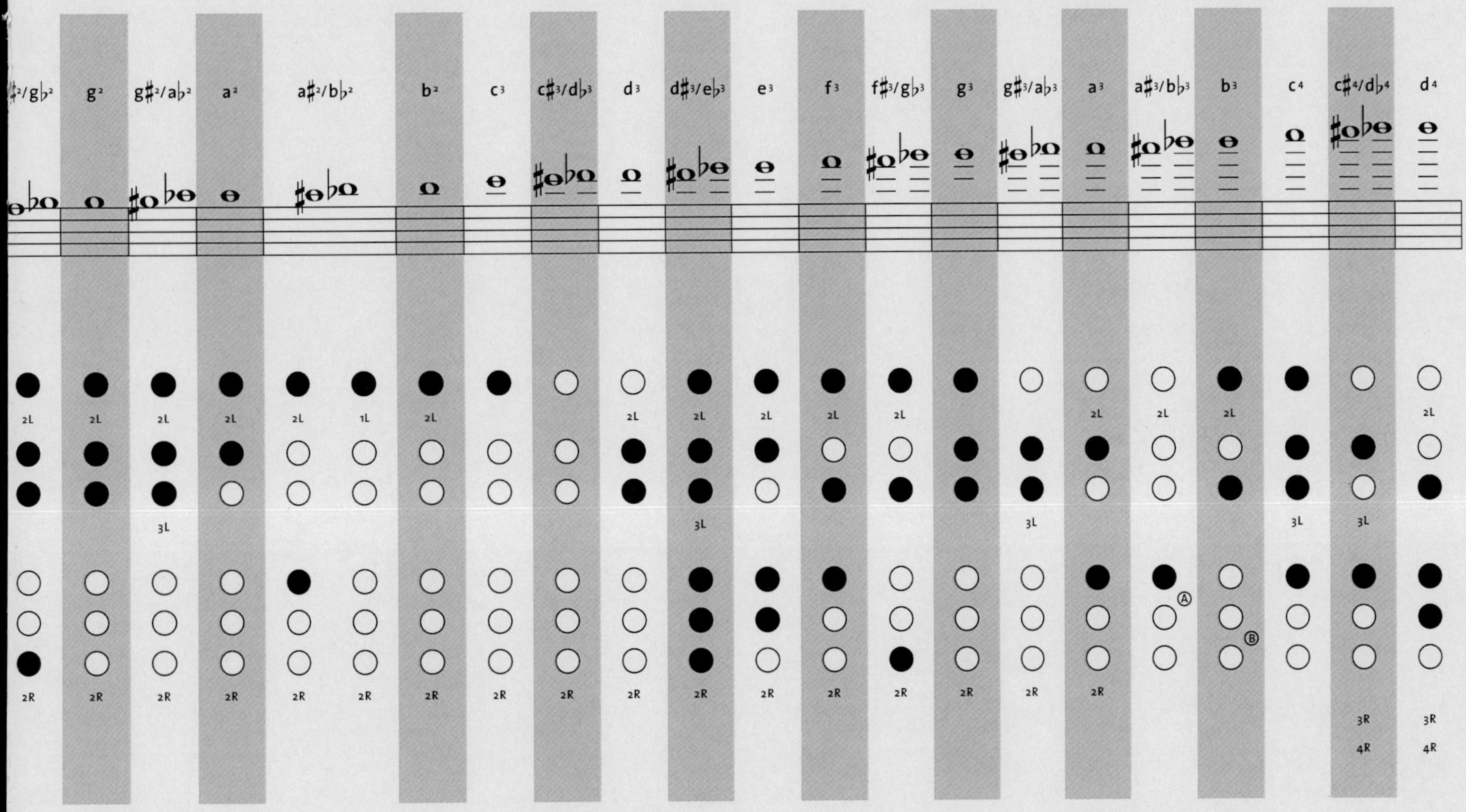
♯2/g♭2
g2
g♯2/a♭2
a2
a♯2/b♭2
b2
c3
c♯3/d♭3
d3
d♯3/e♭3
e3
f3
f♯3/g♭3
g3
g♯3/a♭3
a3
a♯3/b♭3
b3
c4
c♯4/d♭4
d4

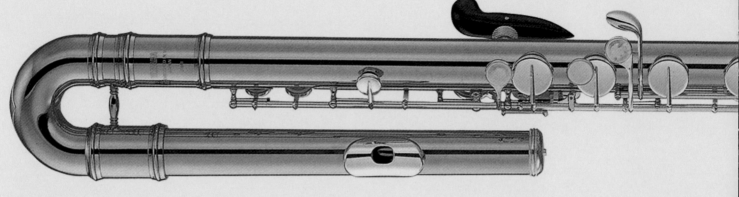

Bass Flute

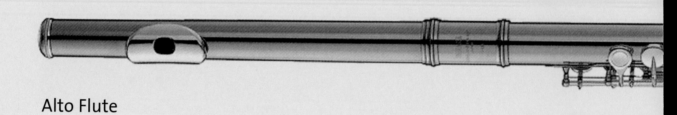

Alto Flute

Flute

Practical Ranges of the Flute Family

written

sounds

Bass Flute   Alto Flute   Flute   Piccolo

Pictures courtsey of Yamaha-Kemble Music

Pieces for Lesson 28

Moment Musical

Schubert

39-40

No triplets to worry about here. However, there are plenty of acciaccaturas.

goals:

1. Improving your tone
2. Breath control
3. More dynamics

Improving your tone

There must have been something about the flute that made you want to learn to play one. When played by an expert, it has a unique sound that can make the hair on the back of your neck stand on end.

Try to record yourself playing one of your favourite pieces from this book. You don't have to hire a recording studio: most computers can record sound, and schools and colleges often have a good recording device.

Listen to the recording. How do you sound compared to your teacher or your favourite flute player on CD? A great tone takes years to develop. It is not just knowing what to do, it is also building up muscles and stamina, just like an athlete would to compete at the highest level.

The following *tone exercises* could be thought of as your flute gym routine.
The more you play these exercises, the better you will sound.

Practise in front of a mirror to check for a relaxed posture, correct embouchure and good hand position. Try to spend five to ten minutes, three times a week, on this routine.

Tone exercise 1:

Breathe in slowly and deeply. Play the first note for a count of 4. Slur to the lower note and hold it on for as long as possible using your diaphragm, which will support the sound.

Relax, breathe in slowly, and play the next pair.

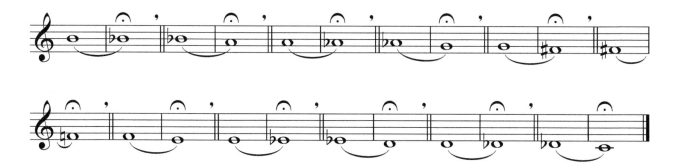

This exercise is to:

- Build muscles so you can keep your throat open and relaxed at all times when playing

- Enlarge your lung capacity and control your airflow using your diaphragm

Tone exercise 2:

Breathe when you need to for this exercise. Play this very slowly but in tempo. Do not get louder the higher you go, and be careful with your intonation. You will need to control the direction of your air very carefully with this exercise.

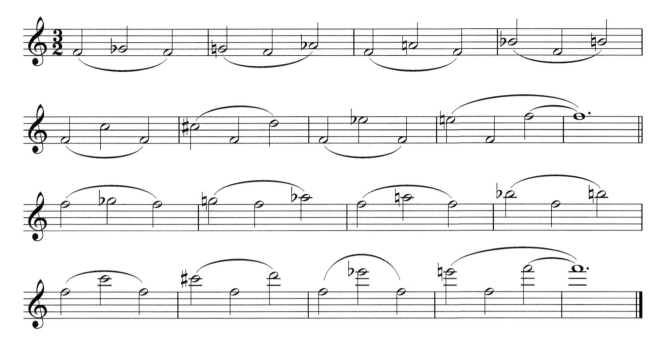

This exercise is to:

- Improve evenness throughout the octaves
- Increase flexibility and accuracy of embouchure
- Improve reliability of intonation

Dynamic Extremes

Up till now you have played music with dynamics ranging anywhere from quiet to loud (p to f).
As your strength and control increases, you could be asked to play very quiet (*pianissimo*) pp, or very loud (*fortissimo*) ff

Tone exercise 3:

Breathe in slowly and deeply. Play each note for as long as you can, moving very slowly and perfectly smoothly through the dynamics as indicated (as though turning a volume knob). You will need to alter your diaphragm support as well as your embouchure according to the dynamic marking.
Be careful not to go sharp as you get louder.

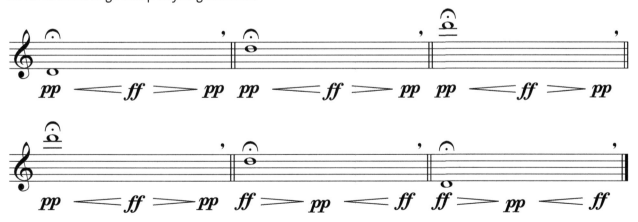

This exercise is to:

- Increase your diaphragm control
- Improve awareness of embouchure
- Improve your intonation

Pieces for Lesson 29

Adagietto from Symphony No. 5

Mahler

This should be slow, and very expressive. It ranks among the most passionate music ever written.

goals:

1. **The note top F♯**
2. **Practice routine**
3. **Trills**

Top F♯

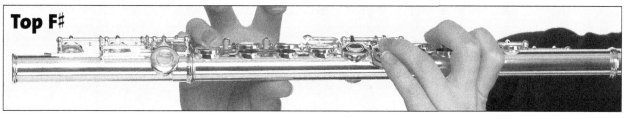

Top F♯

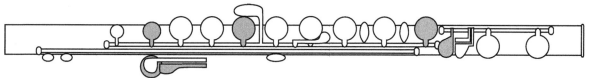

Exercise 1:

F♯ is a hard note to play. A perfect embouchure is needed for the note to sound.

Practice routine

There is one basic fact that applies to playing every musical instrument: **the more you practise, the quicker you will improve**. Some people enjoy practising and others don't. However, a fixed daily routine is essential to make the best of your time.

- Try to practise at the same time every day
- Be focussed: keep your mind entirely on your practice
- Remember your targets for the week (new pieces, scales etc)
- Spend good time on technical work; don't just play your pieces
- Don't be impatient: remember that you will be a better player for having practised

Use the following table to log your practice for this week.

Be honest...this is to help *you* work out how to improve at a quicker pace.

Day	Long note warm ups	Tone *or* Intonation Exercise		Scales	Pieces	Total minutes
		Tone	**Intonation**			

Trills

Although usually found in music from the Baroque era (1600-1750) and the Classical era (1750-1820), trills are a very important form of ornamentation in many styles of music. The written note is rapidly alternated with the note above:

Not exact semiquavers, just as fast as possible.

For music written before 1750, begin the trill on the upper note.

Pieces for Lesson 30

42-43

Gavotte from Suite No. 3

J. S. Bach (1685-1750)

Look at Bach's dates: on which notes do the trills begin?

Pieces for Lesson 30

Minuetto from Eine Kleine Nachtmusik   W. A. Mozart (1756-1791)

This is from the late 18th Century. Play all repeats, then go back to the sign and play to *Fine*, this time without repeating.

44-45

Lesson 31 goals:

1. Rubato
2. Solo playing

Rubato

Sometimes, subtly altering the tempo during a piece of music can be very expressive.
Soloists often use a kind of hesitation, or slowing down, to achieve a dramatic effect.
This is known as *rubato* (Italian for 'robbed') and is especially effective when used sparingly.

Originally rubato passages 'borrowed' time by slowing down, and then caught up with the accompaniment by speeding up later in the phrase. Nowadays playing rubato simply means being flexible with the tempo of the performance to create expression.

Solo playing

A good soloist will know the music by heart. This gives the performer confidence and helps the music to flow much more convincingly.

In most music exams, an unaccompanied piece tests your ability to play *solo*.
You may also be asked to perform in a concert, or you may want to play
for your friends and family.

A guide for solo playing

• If the piece has a lively rhythm, it is essential that you keep the beat steady. Music is a language, and if people can tap their toes to what you are playing, you are communicating with them.

• Never perform a piece so fast that you have to slow down for the tricky passages. Practise everything at one tempo and gradually speed up the whole piece.

• If the piece is dreamier in nature, then allow yourself some rubato. Enjoy the feeling of power that you can control your audience. Make them wait for expressive moments, or increase their excitement by pushing the tempo a little faster.

• Whatever the piece, always think before you play. Try to hear the beginning of the piece in your head... breathe... breathe again... then play.

Solo Pieces for Lesson 31

Sailor's Hornpipe
English folk dance

Traditionally this piece begins very slowly and gradually builds up tempo to a fast, rousing conclusion.
However, make sure you can play it all perfectly at a moderate tempo before you try anything fancy.

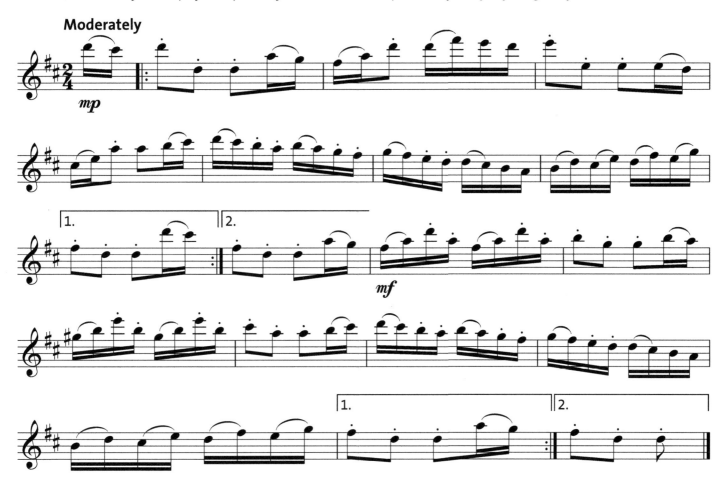

Sometimes I Feel Like A Motherless Child
Spiritual

Here's an opportunity for rubato. Learn the piece keeping to a strict, slow tempo. Then think how you might
make it more expressive by changing this at times.

46

Solo Pieces for Lesson 31

100% Humidity

Ned Bennett

47

Swing this piece which uses the G Blues scale. Keep the tempo steady (no *rubato*), and repeat the improvisation section as many times as you like. You must always relate the notes to the beat which should remain implied by what you play. Take the ideas for your improvisation from the written music if you wish.

Medium Shuffle

(G Blues scale)

goals:

**1. Simple time, compound time,
   and unusual time signatures**
2. More scales

Lesson
32

Time signatures

In *simple* time signatures the beat can be divided into two. It means that the music flows predictably and this is why these signatures are the most commonly found:

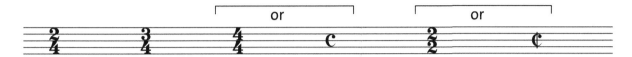

In *compound* time signatures the beat divides into three. The music still flows well.

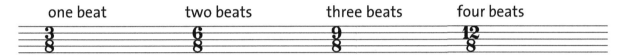

All the pieces that you have played so far in this book use a time signature from the illustrations above. However, many pieces deliberately use a less-flowing time signature:

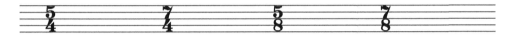

Exercise 1:

Clap the following examples, emphasising the notes on which accents have been placed.

By the way, the time signature may change at any point in a piece! Have a look at the *Bulgarian Dance* later in this lesson to see an example of this.

Exercise 2: New scales and arpeggios

Scale:

G major
two octaves

Arpeggio:

B minor
a twelfth

*Play these according
to the time signatures
and accents
(although normally
you should play them
with equal weighting
for each note).*

Scale:

Arpeggio:

Pieces for Lesson 32

48-49

Bulgarian Dance

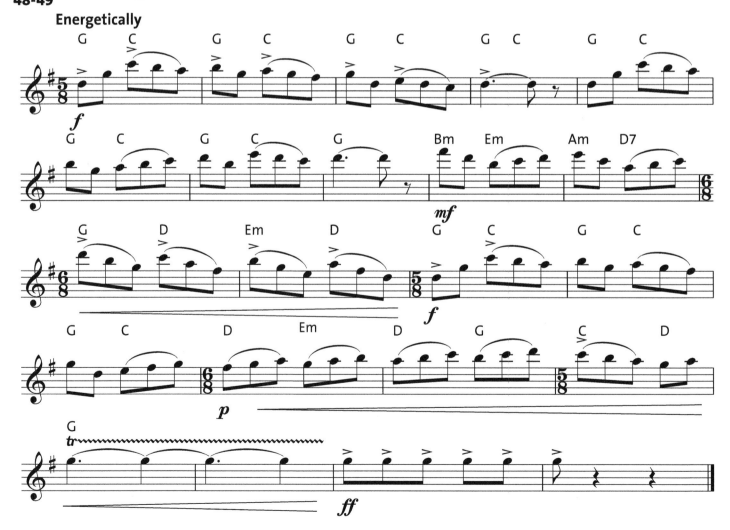

Pieces for Lesson 32

Ut tuo propitiatus

At first this piece may sound odd, perhaps rather modern and experimental, even though it was written almost a thousand years ago.

Try to find a church or large hall with lots of reverberation in which to play it. Originally this would have been sung by monks. However, the sound of two flutes can be equally as haunting.

Don't play this fast, and stick like glue to the tempo until the very end.

Lesson 33 goals:

1. Dexterity
2. Articulation

Dexterity

You may have listened to a piece of music that is so fast you can hardly hear the individual notes.
When played well, this can sound impressive and exciting. However, it takes a long time and endless patience
to develop the skill needed to play very quickly.

Exercise 1:

Practise these exercises regularly, instead of (or in addition to) your intonation and tone exercises.

This exercise uses patterns of the first three notes of every major scale. Make sure you spend more time with
the patterns you can't play very well in order to play the whole exercise at a reasonable tempo, both slurred
and tongued (which is hard!).

The first key has been written out in full. Play the rest in the same manner.

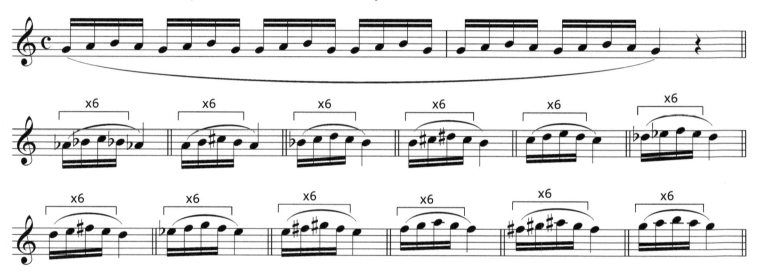

Exercise 2:

This one is chromatic and happens to work down through the keys, but you could equally work up.
Follow the articulation carefully (slurs, tongued notes and staccatos), keeping the sound as clean as you can.

Pieces for Lesson 33

Caprice No. 24 (theme)

Paganini

50

Presto means fast. This piece was originally written for violin, but it has been arranged for piano, cello, and jazz band as well as flute.

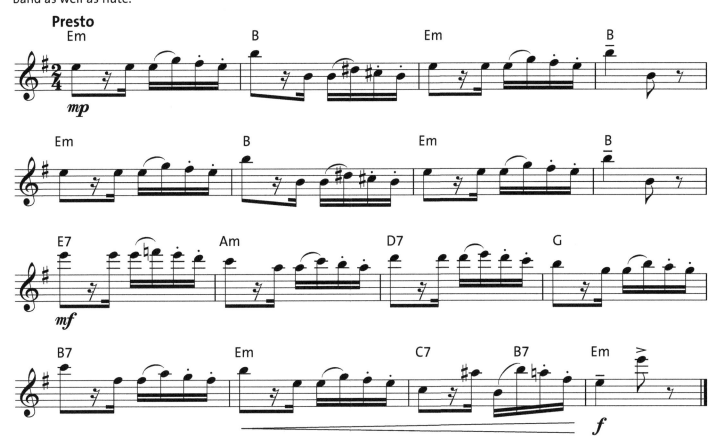

The Irish Washer Woman

Irish 18th Century

51

Coordination between your tongue and fingers is essential for this piece.

Pieces for Lesson 33

52-53

Czardas

Monti

Play the first (slow) section with just a little rubato. The second section needs to be very fast.

As with all fast music, practise it slowly but in tempo otherwise you will never learn the correct timing.

goals:

1. Endurance
2. Sensitivity

Playing for any length of time puts a strain on certain muscles. Think of running an 800 metre race. The first lap is usually okay, but you will feel the pain in your legs during the second lap. This is because when you tighten your muscles, blood can not flow through them and *lactic acid* builds up. Your embouchure muscles go through the same process in a long piece.

It is important to keep your entire body relaxed when you play.

Don't forget to be sensitive to the other musicians. In this piece you will sometimes have an interesting melody, but sometimes you will be accompanying other players. Adjust your dynamic level (volume) to reflect this during this 16th century masterpiece.

Alla riva del Tebro (madrigal)
Palestrina

Although the notes in this quartet seem easy, playing it will be hard. Make sure you count like crazy.
If you get lost you will find it almost impossible to find your place again.

1. Concert Performing

Concert Performing

Having worked through books 1 and 2 of *A New Tune A Day*, you should be ready to perform as part of a concert, whether for friends and family, at school, or for an audience you've never met.

Give yourself the best chance of success with these golden rules.

1 Know your music.
You must be able to play all your pieces, perfectly and without thinking. Musicians play much better if they have memorised the music.

2 Look the part.
Dress smartly, and present yourself as you would for meeting someone very important. This will help you to feel confident when you play.

3 Breathe slowly and deeply before you play.
This will help overcome nerves, and oxygenate your brain helping you to concentrate. It also lets you pause to think about the pulse.

4 Bow slowly to the audience when they clap.
This is good manners, as if to say "thank you for listening to me".

Pieces for Lesson 35

The following pieces are all great for a performance. Even if you are playing them just for practice or fun, imagine you are giving a live performance and play with all the expression, technique and accuracy you can.

Wedding Dance

Kazakstan

54-55   Here is a fiddly melody with many complications, but rewarding to play if you practise it carefully.

Energetic

E and B ped. accomp.

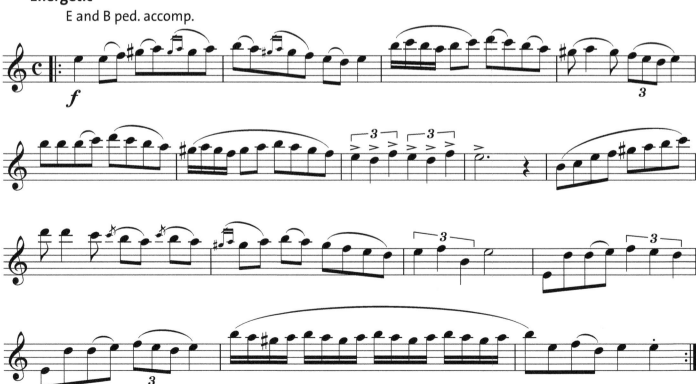

Pieces for Lesson 35

Waltz from Die Fledermaus

Strauss

56-57

This is a fine, flowing waltz that needs lots of energy to perform.

This piece is always performed as part of the New Year's Day concert in Vienna, Austria.

Pieces for Lesson 35

Oh, Won't You Sit Down

Spiritual.

58-59

This piece has been arranged in a jazz style. Play swing quavers, and instead of the written notes, play a D Blues scale improvisation in the section marked *solo ad lib* if you prefer.

Pieces for Lesson 35

Hungarian Dance No. 5

Brahms

60-61

Finally, an exciting romp to finish the book. Watch out for the tempo changes towards the end, and make sure your fingers know the notes by themselves.

Audio backing tracks